CAMPING JC

and RV Travel Logbook

making ★ *memories*

ONE CAMPSITE *at a time*

This book belongs to:

_____

Journal # _____

From: ____/____/_____   To: ____/____/_____

Table of Contents

States Visited

X	State	X	State	X	State
	Alabama		Louisiana		Ohio
	Alaska		Maine		Oklahoma
	Arizona		Maryland		Oregon
	Arkansas		Massachusetts		Pennsylvania
	California		Michigan		Rhode Island
	Colorado		Minnesota		South Carolina
	Connecticut		Mississippi		South Dakota
	Delaware		Missouri		Tennessee
	Florida		Montana		Texas
	Georgia		Nebraska		Utah
	Hawaii		Nevada		Vermont
	Idaho		New Hampshire		Virginia
	Illinois		New Jersey		Washington
	Indiana		New Mexico		West Virginia
	Iowa		New York		Wisconsin
	Kansas		North Carolina		Wyoming
	Kentucky		North Dakota		District of Columbia

From: _____

To: _____

Route taken: _____

_____

Location: _____

Start		End		Total Miles Traveled	

Weather : ☀️ ⛅ ☁️ 🌧️ ⛈️ ❄️

○ ○ ○ ○ ○ ○

CAMPGROUND INFORMATION

Name: _____

Address: _____

Phone: _____

Site: # _____ $ _____

Day	Week	Month

	First Visit		Return Visit		Easy Access		
	Site Level		Back in		Pull through		
	15 amp		30 amp		50 amp		
	Water		Sewer		Shade		Sun
	Paved		Sand/Grass		Gravel		
	Picnic Table		Fire Ring		Trees		Lawn
	Patio		Kid Friendly		Pet Friendly		
	Store		Cafe		Firewood		
	Ice		Security		Quiet		Noisy

GPS: _____

Altitude: _____

Cell Service/Carrier: _____

Wifi Available ○ Free ○ Fee $ _____

Memberships: _____

Amenities: _____

Location
😊 🙂 🙁 😠

Restrooms/Showers
😊 🙂 🙁 😠

Laundry
😊 🙂 🙁 😠

Pool
😊 🙂 🙁 😠

Hot tub
😊 🙂 🙁 😠

Overall rating
☆ ☆ ☆ ☆ ☆

Notes

Highlights & Favorite Things

Places & Activities:

Contacts/New Friends

Name	Phone	E-mail	Mailing Address

Journal Page

Journal Page

From: _____
To: _____
Route taken: _____
_____

Location: _____

Start		End		Total Miles Traveled	

Weather : ☀ ⛅ ☁ 🌧 ⛈ ❄
○ ○ ○ ○ ○ ○

CAMPGROUND INFORMATION

Name: _____
Address: _____
Phone: _____
Site: # _____ $ _____

Day	Week	Month

	First Visit		Return Visit		Easy Access		
	Site Level		Back in		Pull through		
	15 amp		30 amp		50 amp		
	Water		Sewer		Shade		Sun
	Paved		Sand/Grass		Gravel		
	Picnic Table		Fire Ring		Trees		Lawn
	Patio		Kid Friendly		Pet Friendly		
	Store		Cafe		Firewood		
	Ice		Security		Quiet		Noisy

GPS: _____
Altitude: _____
Cell Service/Carrier: _____

Wifi Available ○ Free ○ Fee $ _____

Memberships: _____
Amenities: _____

Location
😃 🙂 🙁 😠

Restrooms/Showers
😃 🙂 🙁 😠

Laundry
😃 🙂 🙁 😠

Pool
😃 🙂 🙁 😠

Hot tub
😃 🙂 🙁 😠

Overall rating
☆ ☆ ☆ ☆ ☆

Notes

Highlights & Favorite Things

Places & Activities:

Contacts/New Friends

Name	Phone	E-mail	Mailing Address

Journal Page

Journal Page

From: _____

To: _____

Route taken: _____

_____

Date: _____

Location: _____

Start		End		Total Miles Traveled	

Weather : ☀ ⛅ ☁ 🌧 ⛈ ❄

○　　○　　○　　○　　○　　○

CAMPGROUND INFORMATION

Name: _____

Address: _____

Phone: _____

Site: # _____ $ _____

Day	Week	Month

	First Visit		Return Visit		Easy Access
	Site Level		Back in		Pull through
	15 amp		30 amp		50 amp
	Water		Sewer		Shade	☐ Sun
	Paved		Sand/Grass		Gravel
	Picnic Table		Fire Ring		Trees	☐ Lawn
	Patio		Kid Friendly		Pet Friendly
	Store		Cafe		Firewood
	Ice		Security		Quiet	☐ Noisy

GPS: _____

Altitude: _____

Cell Service/Carrier: _____

Wifi Available ○ Free ○ Fee $ _____

Memberships: _____

Amenities: _____

Location
😀 🙂 🙁 😠

Restrooms/Showers
😀 🙂 🙁 😠

Laundry
😀 🙂 🙁 😠

Pool
😀 🙂 🙁 😠

Hot tub
😀 🙂 🙁 😠

Overall rating
☆ ☆ ☆ ☆ ☆

Notes

Highlights & Favorite Things

Places & Activities:

Contacts/New Friends

Name	Phone	E-mail	Mailing Address

Journal Page

Journal Page

From: ───────────────────

To: ───────────────────

Date:

Route taken: ─────────────────

─────────────────────────

Location: ───────────────────

Start		End		Total Miles Traveled	

Weather : ☀ ○ ⛅ ○ ☁ ○ 🌧 ○ ⛈ ○ ❄ ○

CAMPGROUND INFORMATION

Name: ─────────────────

Address: ─────────────────

Phone: ─────────────────

Site: # ────── $ ──────

	Day	Week	Month

☐ First Visit	☐ Return Visit	☐ Easy Access			
☐ Site Level	☐ Back in	☐ Pull through			
☐ 15 amp	☐ 30 amp	☐ 50 amp			
☐ Water	☐ Sewer	☐ Shade	☐ Sun		
☐ Paved	☐ Sand/Grass	☐ Gravel			
☐ Picnic Table	☐ Fire Ring	☐ Trees	☐ Lawn		
☐ Patio	☐ Kid Friendly	☐ Pet Friendly			
☐ Store	☐ Cafe	☐ Firewood			
☐ Ice	☐ Security	☐ Quiet	☐ Noisy		

GPS: ─────────────────

Altitude: ─────────────────

Cell Service/Carrier: ─────────────

Wifi Available ○ Free ○ Fee $ ─────

Memberships: ─────────────────

Amenities: ─────────────────

Location
🙂 🙂 🙁 😠

Restrooms/Showers
🙂 🙂 🙁 😠

Laundry
🙂 🙂 🙁 😠

Pool
🙂 🙂 🙁 😠

Hot tub
🙂 🙂 🙁 😠

Overall rating
☆ ☆ ☆ ☆ ☆

Notes

_____

_____

Highlights & Favorite Things

_____

_____

Places & Activities:

_____

_____

_____

_____

_____

Contacts/New Friends

Name	Phone	E-mail	Mailing Address

Journal Page

Journal Page

From: _____
To: _____

Date: _____

Route taken: _____
_____

Location: _____

Start		End		Total Miles Traveled	

Weather : ☀ ⛅ ☁ 🌧 ⛈ ❄
○ ○ ○ ○ ○ ○

CAMPGROUND INFORMATION

Name: _____
Address: _____
Phone: _____
Site: # _____ $ _____

	Day	Week	Month

	First Visit		Return Visit		Easy Access
	Site Level		Back in		Pull through
	15 amp		30 amp		50 amp
	Water		Sewer		Shade	Sun
	Paved		Sand/Grass		Gravel
	Picnic Table		Fire Ring		Trees	Lawn
	Patio		Kid Friendly		Pet Friendly
	Store		Cafe		Firewood
	Ice		Security		Quiet	Noisy

GPS: _____
Altitude: _____
Cell Service/Carrier: _____

Wifi Available ○ Free ○ Fee $ _____

Memberships: _____
Amenities: _____

Location
😀 🙂 🙁 😠

Restrooms/Showers
😀 🙂 🙁 😠

Laundry
😀 🙂 🙁 😠

Pool
😀 🙂 🙁 😠

Hot tub
😀 🙂 🙁 😠

Overall rating
☆ ☆ ☆ ☆ ☆

Notes

Highlights & Favorite Things

Places & Activities:

Contacts/New Friends

Name	Phone	E-mail	Mailing Address

Journal Page

Journal Page

From: _____
To: _____

Date: _____

Route taken: _____
_____

Location: _____

Start		End		Total Miles Traveled	

Weather : ☀ ⛅ ☁ 🌧 ⛈ ❄

○ ○ ○ ○ ○ ○

CAMPGROUND INFORMATION

Name: _____
Address: _____
Phone: _____
Site: # _____ $ _____

Day	Week	Month

	First Visit		Return Visit		Easy Access
	Site Level		Back in		Pull through
	15 amp		30 amp		50 amp
	Water		Sewer		Shade	☐ Sun
	Paved		Sand/Grass		Gravel
	Picnic Table		Fire Ring		Trees	☐ Lawn
	Patio		Kid Friendly		Pet Friendly
	Store		Cafe		Firewood
	Ice		Security		Quiet	☐ Noisy

GPS: _____
Altitude: _____
Cell Service/Carrier: _____

Wifi Available ○ Free ○ Fee $ _____

Memberships: _____
Amenities: _____

Location
🙂 🙂 🙁 😠

Restrooms/Showers
🙂 🙂 🙁 😠

Laundry
🙂 🙂 🙁 😠

Pool
🙂 🙂 🙁 😠

Hot tub
🙂 🙂 🙁 😠

Overall rating
☆ ☆ ☆ ☆ ☆

Notes

Highlights & Favorite Things

Places & Activities:

Contacts/New Friends

Name	Phone	E-mail	Mailing Address

Journal Page

Journal Page

From: _____

To: _____

Route taken: _____

_____

Date:

Location: _____

| Start | | End | | Total Miles Traveled | |

Weather : ☀ ⛅ ☁ 🌧 ⛈ ❄

○ ○ ○ ○ ○ ○

CAMPGROUND INFORMATION

Name: _____

Address: _____

Phone: _____

Site: # _____ $ _____

| Day | Week | Month |

	First Visit		Return Visit		Easy Access
	Site Level		Back in		Pull through
	15 amp		30 amp		50 amp
	Water		Sewer		Shade		Sun
	Paved		Sand/Grass		Gravel
	Picnic Table		Fire Ring		Trees		Lawn
	Patio		Kid Friendly		Pet Friendly
	Store		Cafe		Firewood
	Ice		Security		Quiet		Noisy

GPS: _____

Altitude: _____

Cell Service/Carrier: _____

Wifi Available ○ Free ○ Fee $ _____

Memberships: _____

Amenities: _____

Location
😃 🙂 🙁 😠

Restrooms/Showers
😃 🙂 🙁 😠

Laundry
😃 🙂 🙁 😠

Pool
😃 🙂 🙁 😠

Hot tub
😃 🙂 🙁 😠

Overall rating
☆ ☆ ☆ ☆ ☆

Notes

Highlights & Favorite Things

Places & Activities:

Contacts/New Friends

Name	Phone	E-mail	Mailing Address

Journal Page

Journal Page

From: _____
To: _____

Date: _____

Route taken: _____
_____

Location: _____

Start		End		Total Miles Traveled	

Weather : ☀ ⛅ ☁ 🌧 ⛈ ❄
○ ○ ○ ○ ○ ○

CAMPGROUND INFORMATION

Name: _____

Address: _____

Phone: _____

Site: # _____ $ _____ | Day | Week | Month |

	First Visit		Return Visit		Easy Access	
	Site Level		Back in		Pull through	
	15 amp		30 amp		50 amp	
	Water		Sewer		Shade	☐ Sun
	Paved		Sand/Grass		Gravel	
	Picnic Table		Fire Ring		Trees	☐ Lawn
	Patio		Kid Friendly		Pet Friendly	
	Store		Cafe		Firewood	
	Ice		Security		Quiet	☐ Noisy

GPS: _____

Altitude: _____

Cell Service/Carrier: _____

Wifi Available ○ Free ○ Fee $ _____

Memberships: _____

Amenities: _____

Location
😀 🙂 🙁 😠

Restrooms/Showers
😀 🙂 🙁 😠

Laundry
😀 🙂 🙁 😠

Pool
😀 🙂 🙁 😠

Hot tub
😀 🙂 🙁 😠

Overall rating
☆ ☆ ☆ ☆ ☆

Notes

Highlights & Favorite Things

Places & Activities:

Contacts/New Friends

Name	Phone	E-mail	Mailing Address

Journal Page

Journal Page

From: _____

To: _____

Date:

Route taken: _____

_____

Location: _____

Start		End		Total Miles Traveled	

Weather : ☀ ⛅ ☁ 🌧 ⛈ ❄

○ ○ ○ ○ ○ ○

CAMPGROUND INFORMATION

Name: _____

Address: _____

Phone: _____

Site: # _____ $ _____ | Day | Week | Month |

	First Visit		Return Visit		Easy Access	
	Site Level		Back in		Pull through	
	15 amp		30 amp		50 amp	
	Water		Sewer		Shade	Sun
	Paved		Sand/Grass		Gravel	
	Picnic Table		Fire Ring		Trees	Lawn
	Patio		Kid Friendly		Pet Friendly	
	Store		Cafe		Firewood	
	Ice		Security		Quiet	Noisy

GPS: _____

Altitude: _____

Cell Service/Carrier: _____

Wifi Available ○ Free ○ Fee $ _____

Memberships: _____

Amenities: _____

Location
😃 🙂 🙁 😠

Restrooms/Showers
😃 🙂 🙁 😠

Laundry
😃 🙂 🙁 😠

Pool
😃 🙂 🙁 😠

Hot tub
😃 🙂 🙁 😠

Overall rating
☆ ☆ ☆ ☆ ☆

Notes

Highlights & Favorite Things

Places & Activities:

Contacts/New Friends

Name	Phone	E-mail	Mailing Address

Journal Page

Journal Page

From: _____

To: _____

Route taken: _____

_____

Date: _____

Location: _____

Start		End		Total Miles Traveled	

Weather : ☀ ○ ⛅ ○ ☁ ○ 🌧 ○ ⛈ ○ ❄ ○

CAMPGROUND INFORMATION

Name: _____

Address: _____

Phone: _____

Site: # _____ $ _____

Day	Week	Month

☐	First Visit	☐	Return Visit	☐	Easy Access		
☐	Site Level	☐	Back in	☐	Pull through		
☐	15 amp	☐	30 amp	☐	50 amp		
☐	Water	☐	Sewer	☐	Shade	☐	Sun
☐	Paved	☐	Sand/Grass	☐	Gravel		
☐	Picnic Table	☐	Fire Ring	☐	Trees	☐	Lawn
☐	Patio	☐	Kid Friendly	☐	Pet Friendly		
☐	Store	☐	Cafe	☐	Firewood		
☐	Ice	☐	Security	☐	Quiet	☐	Noisy

GPS: _____

Altitude: _____

Cell Service/Carrier: _____

Wifi Available ○ Free ○ Fee $ _____

Memberships: _____

Amenities: _____

Location
😀 🙂 🙁 😠

Restrooms/Showers
😀 🙂 🙁 😠

Laundry
😀 🙂 🙁 😠

Pool
😀 🙂 🙁 😠

Hot tub
😀 🙂 🙁 😠

Overall rating
☆ ☆ ☆ ☆ ☆

Notes

Highlights & Favorite Things

Places & Activities:

Contacts/New Friends

Name	Phone	E-mail	Mailing Address

Journal Page

Journal Page

From: _____

To: _____

Route taken: _____

_____

Date: _____

Location: _____

Start		End		Total Miles Traveled	

Weather : ☀ ⛅ ☁ 🌧 ⛈ ❄
○ ○ ○ ○ ○ ○

CAMPGROUND INFORMATION

Name: _____

Address: _____

Phone: _____

Site: # _____ $ _____ | Day | Week | Month |

☐ First Visit	☐ Return Visit	☐ Easy Access	
☐ Site Level	☐ Back in	☐ Pull through	
☐ 15 amp	☐ 30 amp	☐ 50 amp	
☐ Water	☐ Sewer	☐ Shade	☐ Sun
☐ Paved	☐ Sand/Grass	☐ Gravel	
☐ Picnic Table	☐ Fire Ring	☐ Trees	☐ Lawn
☐ Patio	☐ Kid Friendly	☐ Pet Friendly	
☐ Store	☐ Cafe	☐ Firewood	
☐ Ice	☐ Security	☐ Quiet	☐ Noisy

GPS: _____

Altitude: _____

Cell Service/Carrier: _____

Wifi Available ○ Free ○ Fee $ _____

Memberships: _____

Amenities: _____

Location
🙂 🙂 🙁 😠

Restrooms/Showers
🙂 🙂 🙁 😠

Laundry
🙂 🙂 🙁 😠

Pool
🙂 🙂 🙁 😠

Hot tub
🙂 🙂 🙁 😠

Overall rating
☆ ☆ ☆ ☆ ☆

Notes

Highlights & Favorite Things

Places & Activities:

Contacts/New Friends

Name	Phone	E-mail	Mailing Address

Journal Page

Journal Page

From: _____

To: _____

Date: _____

Route taken: _____

_____

Location: _____

Start		End		Total Miles Traveled	

Weather : ☀ ⛅ ☁ 🌧 ⛈ ❄

○ ○ ○ ○ ○ ○

CAMPGROUND INFORMATION

Name: _____

Address: _____

Phone: _____

Site: # _____ $ _____

Day	Week	Month

☐ First Visit	☐ Return Visit	☐ Easy Access			
☐ Site Level	☐ Back in	☐ Pull through			
☐ 15 amp	☐ 30 amp	☐ 50 amp			
☐ Water	☐ Sewer	☐ Shade	☐ Sun		
☐ Paved	☐ Sand/Grass	☐ Gravel			
☐ Picnic Table	☐ Fire Ring	☐ Trees	☐ Lawn		
☐ Patio	☐ Kid Friendly	☐ Pet Friendly			
☐ Store	☐ Cafe	☐ Firewood			
☐ Ice	☐ Security	☐ Quiet	☐ Noisy		

GPS: _____

Altitude: _____

Cell Service/Carrier: _____

Wifi Available ○ Free ○ Fee $ _____

Memberships: _____

Amenities: _____

Location
😀 🙂 🙁 😠

Restrooms/Showers
😀 🙂 🙁 😠

Laundry
😀 🙂 🙁 😠

Pool
😀 🙂 🙁 😠

Hot tub
😀 🙂 🙁 😠

Overall rating
☆ ☆ ☆ ☆ ☆

Notes

Highlights & Favorite Things

Places & Activities:

Contacts/New Friends

Name	Phone	E-mail	Mailing Address

Journal Page

Journal Page

From: _____

To: _____

Route taken: _____
_____

Date: _____

Location: _____

Start		End		Total Miles Traveled	

Weather : ☀ ⛅ ☁ 🌧 ⛈ ❄
○ ○ ○ ○ ○ ○

CAMPGROUND INFORMATION

Name: _____

Address: _____

Phone: _____

Site: # _____ $ _____

Day	Week	Month

	First Visit		Return Visit		Easy Access		
	Site Level		Back in		Pull through		
	15 amp		30 amp		50 amp		
	Water		Sewer		Shade		Sun
	Paved		Sand/Grass		Gravel		
	Picnic Table		Fire Ring		Trees		Lawn
	Patio		Kid Friendly		Pet Friendly		
	Store		Cafe		Firewood		
	Ice		Security		Quiet		Noisy

GPS: _____

Altitude: _____

Cell Service/Carrier: _____

Wifi Available ○ Free ○ Fee $ _____

Memberships: _____

Amenities: _____

Location
😃 🙂 🙁 😠

Restrooms/Showers
😃 🙂 🙁 😠

Laundry
😃 🙂 🙁 😠

Pool
😃 🙂 🙁 😠

Hot tub
😃 🙂 🙁 😠

Overall rating
☆ ☆ ☆ ☆ ☆

Notes

_____

_____

Highlights & Favorite Things

_____

_____

Places & Activities:

_____

_____

_____

_____

_____

Contacts/New Friends

Name	Phone	E-mail	Mailing Address

Journal Page

Journal Page

From: _____

To: _____

Route taken: _____

_____

Location: _____

Start		End		Total Miles Traveled	

Weather : ☀ ⛅ ☁ 🌧 ⛈ ❄

○ ○ ○ ○ ○ ○

CAMPGROUND INFORMATION

Name: _____

Address: _____

Phone: _____

Site: # _____ $ _____

Day	Week	Month

	First Visit		Return Visit		Easy Access		
	Site Level		Back in		Pull through		
	15 amp		30 amp		50 amp		
	Water		Sewer		Shade	☐	Sun
	Paved		Sand/Grass		Gravel		
	Picnic Table		Fire Ring		Trees	☐	Lawn
	Patio		Kid Friendly		Pet Friendly		
	Store		Cafe		Firewood		
	Ice		Security		Quiet	☐	Noisy

GPS: _____

Altitude: _____

Cell Service/Carrier: _____

Wifi Available ○ Free ○ Fee $ _____

Memberships: _____

Amenities: _____

Location

😀 🙂 🙁 😠

Restrooms/Showers

😀 🙂 🙁 😠

Laundry

😀 🙂 🙁 😠

Pool

😀 🙂 🙁 😠

Hot tub

😀 🙂 🙁 😠

Overall rating

☆ ☆ ☆ ☆ ☆

Notes

Highlights & Favorite Things

Places & Activities:

Contacts/New Friends

Name	Phone	E-mail	Mailing Address

Journal Page

Journal Page

From: _____

To: _____

Route taken: _____

_____

Date: _____

Location: _____

Start		End		Total Miles Traveled	

Weather : ☀ ⛅ ☁ 🌧 ⛈ ❄

○　○　○　○　○　○

CAMPGROUND INFORMATION

Name: _____

Address: _____

Phone: _____

Site: # _____ $ _____ | Day | Week | Month |

	First Visit		Return Visit		Easy Access	
	Site Level		Back in		Pull through	
	15 amp		30 amp		50 amp	
	Water		Sewer		Shade	☐ Sun
	Paved		Sand/Grass		Gravel	
	Picnic Table		Fire Ring		Trees	☐ Lawn
	Patio		Kid Friendly		Pet Friendly	
	Store		Cafe		Firewood	
	Ice		Security		Quiet	☐ Noisy

GPS: _____

Altitude: _____

Cell Service/Carrier: _____

Wifi Available ○ Free ○ Fee $ _____

Memberships: _____

Amenities: _____

Location
😃 🙂 ☹ 😠

Restrooms/Showers
😃 🙂 ☹ 😠

Laundry
😃 🙂 ☹ 😠

Pool
😃 🙂 ☹ 😠

Hot tub
😃 🙂 ☹ 😠

Overall rating
☆ ☆ ☆ ☆ ☆

Notes

_____

_____

Highlights & Favorite Things

_____

_____

Places & Activities:

_____

_____

_____

_____

_____

Contacts/New Friends

Name	Phone	E-mail	Mailing Address

Journal Page

Journal Page

From: _____

To: _____

Date: _____

Route taken: _____

_____

Location: _____

Start		End		Total Miles Traveled	

Weather : ○ ○ ○ ○ ○ ○

CAMPGROUND INFORMATION

Name: _____

Address: _____

Phone: _____

Site: # _____ $ _____

Day	Week	Month

- [ ] First Visit
- [ ] Site Level
- [ ] 15 amp
- [ ] Water
- [ ] Paved
- [ ] Picnic Table
- [ ] Patio
- [ ] Store
- [ ] Ice

- [ ] Return Visit
- [ ] Back in
- [ ] 30 amp
- [ ] Sewer
- [ ] Sand/Grass
- [ ] Fire Ring
- [ ] Kid Friendly
- [ ] Cafe
- [ ] Security

- [ ] Easy Access
- [ ] Pull through
- [ ] 50 amp
- [ ] Shade
- [ ] Gravel
- [ ] Trees
- [ ] Pet Friendly
- [ ] Firewood
- [ ] Quiet

- [ ] Sun
- [ ] Lawn
- [ ] Noisy

GPS: _____

Altitude: _____

Cell Service/Carrier: _____

Wifi Available ○ Free ○ Fee $ _____

Memberships: _____

Amenities: _____

Location

Restrooms/Showers

Laundry

Pool

Hot tub

Overall rating

☆ ☆ ☆ ☆ ☆

Notes

_____

_____

Highlights & Favorite Things

_____

_____

Places & Activities:

_____

_____

_____

_____

_____

Contacts/New Friends

Name	Phone	E-mail	Mailing Address

Journal Page

Journal Page

From: _____

To: _____

Route taken: _____

_____

Location: _____

Date: _____

Start		End		Total Miles Traveled	

Weather : ☀️ ⛅ ☁️ 🌧️ ⛈️ ❄️

○ ○ ○ ○ ○ ○

CAMPGROUND INFORMATION

Name: _____

Address: _____

Phone: _____

Site: # _____ $ _____

	Day	Week	Month

☐ First Visit	☐ Return Visit	☐ Easy Access			
☐ Site Level	☐ Back in	☐ Pull through			
☐ 15 amp	☐ 30 amp	☐ 50 amp			
☐ Water	☐ Sewer	☐ Shade	☐ Sun		
☐ Paved	☐ Sand/Grass	☐ Gravel			
☐ Picnic Table	☐ Fire Ring	☐ Trees	☐ Lawn		
☐ Patio	☐ Kid Friendly	☐ Pet Friendly			
☐ Store	☐ Cafe	☐ Firewood			
☐ Ice	☐ Security	☐ Quiet	☐ Noisy		

GPS: _____

Altitude: _____

Cell Service/Carrier: _____

Wifi Available ○ Free ○ Fee $ _____

Memberships: _____

Amenities: _____

Location
🙂 🙂 🙁 😠

Restrooms/Showers
🙂 🙂 🙁 😠

Laundry
🙂 🙂 🙁 😠

Pool
🙂 🙂 🙁 😠

Hot tub
🙂 🙂 🙁 😠

Overall rating
☆ ☆ ☆ ☆ ☆

Notes

Highlights & Favorite Things

Places & Activities:

Contacts/New Friends

Name	Phone	E-mail	Mailing Address

Journal Page

Journal Page

From: _____

To: _____

Date:

Route taken: _____

_____

Location: _____

Start		End		Total Miles Traveled	

Weather : ☀️ ⛅ ☁️ 🌧️ ⛈️ ❄️

○ ○ ○ ○ ○ ○

CAMPGROUND INFORMATION

Name: _____

Address: _____

Phone: _____

Site: # _____ $ _____

Day	Week	Month

	First Visit		Return Visit		Easy Access		
	Site Level		Back in		Pull through		
	15 amp		30 amp		50 amp		
	Water		Sewer		Shade		Sun
	Paved		Sand/Grass		Gravel		
	Picnic Table		Fire Ring		Trees		Lawn
	Patio		Kid Friendly		Pet Friendly		
	Store		Cafe		Firewood		
	Ice		Security		Quiet		Noisy

GPS: _____

Altitude: _____

Cell Service/Carrier: _____

Wifi Available ○ Free ○ Fee $ _____

Memberships: _____

Amenities: _____

Location
😃 🙂 🙁 😠

Restrooms/Showers
😃 🙂 🙁 😠

Laundry
😃 🙂 🙁 😠

Pool
😃 🙂 🙁 😠

Hot tub
😃 🙂 🙁 😠

Overall rating
☆ ☆ ☆ ☆ ☆

Notes

Highlights & Favorite Things

Places & Activities:

Contacts/New Friends

Name	Phone	E-mail	Mailing Address

Journal Page

Journal Page

From: _____

To: _____

Route taken: _____

_____

Location: _____

Start		End		Total Miles Traveled	

Weather : ☐ ☐ ☐ ☐ ☐ ☐

CAMPGROUND INFORMATION

Location

Name: _____

Address: _____

Phone: _____

Site: # _____ $ _____

Restrooms/Showers

	Day	Week	Month

☐ First Visit	☐ Return Visit	☐ Easy Access	
☐ Site Level	☐ Back in	☐ Pull through	
☐ 15 amp	☐ 30 amp	☐ 50 amp	
☐ Water	☐ Sewer	☐ Shade	☐ Sun
☐ Paved	☐ Sand/Grass	☐ Gravel	
☐ Picnic Table	☐ Fire Ring	☐ Trees	☐ Lawn
☐ Patio	☐ Kid Friendly	☐ Pet Friendly	
☐ Store	☐ Cafe	☐ Firewood	
☐ Ice	☐ Security	☐ Quiet	☐ Noisy

Laundry

Pool

GPS: _____

Altitude: _____

Cell Service/Carrier: _____

Hot tub

Wifi Available ◯ Free ◯ Fee $ _____

Memberships: _____

Amenities: _____

Overall rating

☆ ☆ ☆ ☆ ☆

Notes

Highlights & Favorite Things

Places & Activities:

Contacts/New Friends

Name	Phone	E-mail	Mailing Address

Journal Page

Journal Page

From: _____

To: _____

Route taken: _____

_____

Date: _____

Location: _____

Start		End		Total Miles Traveled	

Weather : ☀ ○ ⛅ ○ ☁ ○ 🌧 ○ ⛈ ○ ❄ ○

CAMPGROUND INFORMATION

Name: _____

Address: _____

Phone: _____

Site: # _____ $ _____ | Day | Week | Month |

☐ First Visit	☐ Return Visit	☐ Easy Access			
☐ Site Level	☐ Back in	☐ Pull through			
☐ 15 amp	☐ 30 amp	☐ 50 amp			
☐ Water	☐ Sewer	☐ Shade	☐ Sun		
☐ Paved	☐ Sand/Grass	☐ Gravel			
☐ Picnic Table	☐ Fire Ring	☐ Trees	☐ Lawn		
☐ Patio	☐ Kid Friendly	☐ Pet Friendly			
☐ Store	☐ Cafe	☐ Firewood			
☐ Ice	☐ Security	☐ Quiet	☐ Noisy		

GPS: _____

Altitude: _____

Cell Service/Carrier: _____

Wifi Available ○ Free ○ Fee $ _____

Memberships: _____

Amenities: _____

Location
😃 🙂 🙁 😠

Restrooms/Showers
😃 🙂 🙁 😠

Laundry
😃 🙂 🙁 😠

Pool
😃 🙂 🙁 😠

Hot tub
😃 🙂 🙁 😠

Overall rating
☆ ☆ ☆ ☆ ☆

Notes

Highlights & Favorite Things

Places & Activities:

Contacts/New Friends

Name	Phone	E-mail	Mailing Address

Journal Page

Journal Page

From: _____

To: _____

Date: _____

Route taken: _____

_____

Location: _____

| Start | | End | | Total Miles Traveled | |

Weather : ○ ○ ○ ○ ○ ○

CAMPGROUND INFORMATION

Location

Name: _____

Address: _____

Phone: _____

Site: # _____ $ _____

| Day | Week | Month |

	First Visit		Return Visit		Easy Access
	Site Level		Back in		Pull through
	15 amp		30 amp		50 amp
	Water		Sewer		Shade		Sun
	Paved		Sand/Grass		Gravel
	Picnic Table		Fire Ring		Trees		Lawn
	Patio		Kid Friendly		Pet Friendly
	Store		Cafe		Firewood
	Ice		Security		Quiet		Noisy

GPS: _____

Altitude: _____

Cell Service/Carrier: _____

Wifi Available ○ Free ○ Fee $ _____

Memberships: _____

Amenities: _____

Location

Restrooms/Showers

Laundry

Pool

Hot tub

Overall rating

☆ ☆ ☆ ☆ ☆

Notes

Highlights & Favorite Things

Places & Activities:

Contacts/New Friends

Name	Phone	E-mail	Mailing Address

Journal Page

Journal Page

From: _____
To: _____
Route taken: _____
_____

Date:

Location: _____

Start		End		Total Miles Traveled	

Weather : ○ ○ ○ ○ ○ ○

CAMPGROUND INFORMATION

Name: _____
Address: _____
Phone: _____
Site: # _____ $ _____ | Day | Week | Month |

	First Visit		Return Visit		Easy Access
	Site Level		Back in		Pull through
	15 amp		30 amp		50 amp
	Water		Sewer		Shade
	Paved		Sand/Grass		Gravel
	Picnic Table		Fire Ring		Trees
	Patio		Kid Friendly		Pet Friendly
	Store		Cafe		Firewood
	Ice		Security		Quiet

☐ Sun
☐ Lawn
☐ Noisy

GPS: _____
Altitude: _____
Cell Service/Carrier: _____
Wifi Available ○ Free ○ Fee $ _____
Memberships: _____
Amenities: _____

Location

Restrooms/Showers

Laundry

Pool

Hot tub

Overall rating
☆ ☆ ☆ ☆ ☆

Notes

Highlights & Favorite Things

Places & Activities:

Contacts/New Friends

Name	Phone	E-mail	Mailing Address

Journal Page

Journal Page

From: _____

To: _____

Date:

Route taken: _____

_____

Location: _____

Start		End		Total Miles Traveled	

Weather : ☀ ⛅ ☁ 🌧 ⛈ ❄

○　　○　　○　　○　　○　　○

CAMPGROUND INFORMATION

Name: _____

Address: _____

Phone: _____

Site: # _____ $ _____ | Day | Week | Month |

	First Visit		Return Visit		Easy Access		
	Site Level		Back in		Pull through		
	15 amp		30 amp		50 amp		
	Water		Sewer		Shade	☐	Sun
	Paved		Sand/Grass		Gravel		
	Picnic Table		Fire Ring		Trees	☐	Lawn
	Patio		Kid Friendly		Pet Friendly		
	Store		Cafe		Firewood		
	Ice		Security		Quiet	☐	Noisy

GPS: _____

Altitude: _____

Cell Service/Carrier: _____

Wifi Available ○ Free ○ Fee $ _____

Memberships: _____

Amenities: _____

Location
😃 🙂 🙁 😠

Restrooms/Showers
😃 🙂 🙁 😠

Laundry
😃 🙂 🙁 😠

Pool
😃 🙂 🙁 😠

Hot tub
😃 🙂 🙁 😠

Overall rating
☆ ☆ ☆ ☆ ☆

Notes

_____

_____

Highlights & Favorite Things

_____

_____

Places & Activities:

_____

_____

_____

_____

_____

Contacts/New Friends

Name	Phone	E-mail	Mailing Address

Journal Page

Journal Page

From: _____

To: _____

Route taken: _____

_____

Location: _____

Start		End		Total Miles Traveled	

Weather: ☀ ⛅ ☁ 🌧 ⛈ ❄
○ ○ ○ ○ ○ ○

CAMPGROUND INFORMATION

Name: _____

Address: _____

Phone: _____

Site: # _____ $ _____

Day	Week	Month

	First Visit		Return Visit		Easy Access		
	Site Level		Back in		Pull through		
	15 amp		30 amp		50 amp		
	Water		Sewer		Shade	☐	Sun
	Paved		Sand/Grass		Gravel		
	Picnic Table		Fire Ring		Trees	☐	Lawn
	Patio		Kid Friendly		Pet Friendly		
	Store		Cafe		Firewood		
	Ice		Security		Quiet	☐	Noisy

GPS: _____

Altitude: _____

Cell Service/Carrier: _____

Wifi Available ○ Free ○ Fee $ _____

Memberships: _____

Amenities: _____

Location
😀 🙂 🙁 😠

Restrooms/Showers
😀 🙂 🙁 😠

Laundry
😀 🙂 🙁 😠

Pool
😀 🙂 🙁 😠

Hot tub
😀 🙂 🙁 😠

Overall rating
☆ ☆ ☆ ☆ ☆

Date:

Notes

Highlights & Favorite Things

Places & Activities:

Contacts/New Friends

Name	Phone	E-mail	Mailing Address

Journal Page

Journal Page

From: _____

To: _____

Date:

Route taken: _____

_____

Location: _____

| Start | | End | | Total Miles Traveled | |

Weather : ☀ ⛅ ☁ 🌧 ⛈ ❄
○ ○ ○ ○ ○ ○

CAMPGROUND INFORMATION

Name: _____

Address: _____

Phone: _____

Site: # _____ $ _____ | Day | Week | Month |

	First Visit		Return Visit		Easy Access
	Site Level		Back in		Pull through
	15 amp		30 amp		50 amp
	Water		Sewer		Shade	□ Sun
	Paved		Sand/Grass		Gravel
	Picnic Table		Fire Ring		Trees	□ Lawn
	Patio		Kid Friendly		Pet Friendly
	Store		Cafe		Firewood
	Ice		Security		Quiet	□ Noisy

GPS: _____

Altitude: _____

Cell Service/Carrier: _____

Wifi Available ○ Free ○ Fee $ _____

Memberships: _____

Amenities: _____

Location
🙂 🙂 🙁 😠

Restrooms/Showers
🙂 🙂 🙁 😠

Laundry
🙂 🙂 🙁 😠

Pool
🙂 🙂 🙁 😠

Hot tub
🙂 🙂 🙁 😠

Overall rating
☆ ☆ ☆ ☆ ☆

Notes

Highlights & Favorite Things

Places & Activities:

Contacts/New Friends

Name	Phone	E-mail	Mailing Address

Journal Page

Journal Page

From: _____

To: _____

Date: _____

Route taken: _____

_____

Location: _____

Start		End		Total Miles Traveled	

Weather : ☀ ⛅ ☁ 🌧 ⛈ ❄

○　　○　　○　　○　　○　　○

CAMPGROUND INFORMATION

Name: _____

Address: _____

Phone: _____

Site: # _____ $ _____

Day	Week	Month

☐ First Visit　☐ Return Visit　☐ Easy Access
☐ Site Level　☐ Back in　☐ Pull through
☐ 15 amp　☐ 30 amp　☐ 50 amp
☐ Water　☐ Sewer　☐ Shade　☐ Sun
☐ Paved　☐ Sand/Grass　☐ Gravel
☐ Picnic Table　☐ Fire Ring　☐ Trees　☐ Lawn
☐ Patio　☐ Kid Friendly　☐ Pet Friendly
☐ Store　☐ Cafe　☐ Firewood
☐ Ice　☐ Security　☐ Quiet　☐ Noisy

GPS: _____

Altitude: _____

Cell Service/Carrier: _____

Wifi Available ○ Free ○ Fee $ _____

Memberships: _____

Amenities: _____

Location
🙂 🙂 🙁 😠

Restrooms/Showers
🙂 🙂 🙁 😠

Laundry
🙂 🙂 🙁 😠

Pool
🙂 🙂 🙁 😠

Hot tub
🙂 🙂 🙁 😠

Overall rating
☆ ☆ ☆ ☆ ☆

Notes

_____

_____

Highlights & Favorite Things

_____

_____

Places & Activities:

_____

_____

_____

_____

_____

Contacts/New Friends

Name	Phone	E-mail	Mailing Address

Journal Page

Journal Page

From: _____

To: _____

Route taken: _____
_____

Location: _____

Start		End		Total Miles Traveled	

Weather : ☀ ⛅ ☁ 🌧 ⛈ ❄
○ ○ ○ ○ ○ ○

CAMPGROUND INFORMATION

Name: _____

Address: _____

Phone: _____

Site: # _____ $ _____

Day	Week	Month

	First Visit		Return Visit		Easy Access		
	Site Level		Back in		Pull through		
	15 amp		30 amp		50 amp		
	Water		Sewer		Shade		Sun
	Paved		Sand/Grass		Gravel		
	Picnic Table		Fire Ring		Trees		Lawn
	Patio		Kid Friendly		Pet Friendly		
	Store		Cafe		Firewood		
	Ice		Security		Quiet		Noisy

GPS: _____

Altitude: _____

Cell Service/Carrier: _____

Wifi Available ○ Free ○ Fee $ _____

Memberships: _____

Amenities: _____

Location
😀 🙂 🙁 😠

Restrooms/Showers
😀 🙂 🙁 😠

Laundry
😀 🙂 🙁 😠

Pool
😀 🙂 🙁 😠

Hot tub
😀 🙂 🙁 😠

Overall rating
☆ ☆ ☆ ☆ ☆

Notes

Highlights & Favorite Things

Places & Activities:

Contacts/New Friends

Name	Phone	E-mail	Mailing Address

Journal Page

Journal Page

From: _____

To: _____

Route taken: _____

_____

Location: _____

Date:

| Start | | End | | Total Miles Traveled | |

Weather : ○ ○ ○ ○ ○ ○

CAMPGROUND INFORMATION

Name: _____

Address: _____

Phone: _____

Site: # _____ $ _____

| Day | Week | Month |

	First Visit		Return Visit		Easy Access
	Site Level		Back in		Pull through
	15 amp		30 amp		50 amp
	Water		Sewer		Shade	□ Sun
	Paved		Sand/Grass		Gravel
	Picnic Table		Fire Ring		Trees	□ Lawn
	Patio		Kid Friendly		Pet Friendly
	Store		Cafe		Firewood
	Ice		Security		Quiet	□ Noisy

GPS: _____

Altitude: _____

Cell Service/Carrier: _____

Wifi Available ○ Free ○ Fee $ _____

Memberships: _____

Amenities: _____

Location

Restrooms/Showers

Laundry

Pool

Hot tub

Overall rating

☆ ☆ ☆ ☆ ☆

Notes

_____

_____

Highlights & Favorite Things

_____

_____

Places & Activities:

_____

_____

_____

_____

_____

Contacts/New Friends

Name	Phone	E-mail	Mailing Address

Journal Page

Journal Page

From: _____

To: _____

Date:

Route taken: _____
_____

Location: _____

Start		End		Total Miles Traveled	

Weather : ☀️ ○ ⛅ ○ ☁️ ○ 🌧️ ○ ⛈️ ○ ❄️ ○

CAMPGROUND INFORMATION

Name: _____

Address: _____

Phone: _____

Site: # _____ $ _____

Day	Week	Month

☐ First Visit   ☐ Return Visit   ☐ Easy Access
☐ Site Level   ☐ Back in   ☐ Pull through
☐ 15 amp   ☐ 30 amp   ☐ 50 amp
☐ Water   ☐ Sewer   ☐ Shade   ☐ Sun
☐ Paved   ☐ Sand/Grass   ☐ Gravel
☐ Picnic Table ☐ Fire Ring   ☐ Trees   ☐ Lawn
☐ Patio   ☐ Kid Friendly   ☐ Pet Friendly
☐ Store   ☐ Cafe   ☐ Firewood
☐ Ice   ☐ Security   ☐ Quiet   ☐ Noisy

GPS: _____

Altitude: _____

Cell Service/Carrier: _____

Wifi Available ○ Free ○ Fee $ _____

Memberships: _____

Amenities: _____

Location
😀 🙂 🙁 😠

Restrooms/Showers
😀 🙂 🙁 😠

Laundry
😀 🙂 🙁 😠

Pool
😀 🙂 🙁 😠

Hot tub
😀 🙂 🙁 😠

Overall rating
☆ ☆ ☆ ☆ ☆

Notes

_____

_____

Highlights & Favorite Things

_____

_____

Places & Activities:

_____

_____

_____

_____

Contacts/New Friends

Name	Phone	E-mail	Mailing Address

Journal Page

Journal Page

From: _____

To: _____

Route taken: _____

_____

Date: _____

Location: _____

Start		End		Total Miles Traveled	

Weather : ☀ ○   ⛅ ○   ☁ ○   🌧 ○   ⛈ ○   ❄ ○

CAMPGROUND INFORMATION

Name: _____

Address: _____

Phone: _____

Site: # _____ $ _____

Day	Week	Month

	First Visit		Return Visit		Easy Access
	Site Level		Back in		Pull through
	15 amp		30 amp		50 amp
	Water		Sewer		Shade	☐ Sun
	Paved		Sand/Grass		Gravel
	Picnic Table		Fire Ring		Trees	☐ Lawn
	Patio		Kid Friendly		Pet Friendly
	Store		Cafe		Firewood
	Ice		Security		Quiet	☐ Noisy

GPS: _____

Altitude: _____

Cell Service/Carrier: _____

Wifi Available ○ Free ○ Fee $ _____

Memberships: _____

Amenities: _____

Location
😃 🙂 🙁 😠

Restrooms/Showers
😃 🙂 🙁 😠

Laundry
😃 🙂 🙁 😠

Pool
😃 🙂 🙁 😠

Hot tub
😃 🙂 🙁 😠

Overall rating
☆ ☆ ☆ ☆ ☆

Notes

Highlights & Favorite Things

Places & Activities:

Contacts/New Friends

Name	Phone	E-mail	Mailing Address

Journal Page

Journal Page

From: _____
To: _____
Route taken: _____
_____

Date: _____

Location: _____

Start		End		Total Miles Traveled	

Weather: ☀ ○ ⛅ ○ ☁ ○ 🌧 ○ ⛈ ○ ❄ ○

CAMPGROUND INFORMATION

Name: _____
Address: _____
Phone: _____
Site: # _____ $ _____

Day	Week	Month

	First Visit		Return Visit		Easy Access
	Site Level		Back in		Pull through
	15 amp		30 amp		50 amp
	Water		Sewer		Shade	☐ Sun
	Paved		Sand/Grass		Gravel
	Picnic Table		Fire Ring		Trees	☐ Lawn
	Patio		Kid Friendly		Pet Friendly
	Store		Cafe		Firewood
	Ice		Security		Quiet	☐ Noisy

GPS: _____
Altitude: _____
Cell Service/Carrier: _____

Wifi Available ○ Free ○ Fee $ _____

Memberships: _____
Amenities: _____

Location
😀 🙂 🙁 😠

Restrooms/Showers
😀 🙂 🙁 😠

Laundry
😀 🙂 🙁 😠

Pool
😀 🙂 🙁 😠

Hot tub
😀 🙂 🙁 😠

Overall rating
☆ ☆ ☆ ☆ ☆

Notes

_____

_____

Highlights & Favorite Things

_____

_____

Places & Activities:

_____

_____

_____

_____

_____

Contacts/New Friends

Name	Phone	E-mail	Mailing Address

Journal Page

Journal Page

From: _____

To: _____

Date:

Route taken: _____
_____

Location: _____

Start		End		Total Miles Traveled	

Weather : ☀️ ○ ⛅ ○ ☁️ ○ 🌧️ ○ ⛈️ ○ ❄️ ○

CAMPGROUND INFORMATION

Location

😀 🙂 🙁 😠

Name: _____

Address: _____

Phone: _____

Restrooms/Showers

😀 🙂 🙁 😠

Site: # _____ $ _____

Day	Week	Month

	First Visit		Return Visit		Easy Access
	Site Level		Back in		Pull through
	15 amp		30 amp		50 amp
	Water		Sewer		Shade	☐ Sun
	Paved		Sand/Grass		Gravel
	Picnic Table		Fire Ring		Trees	☐ Lawn
	Patio		Kid Friendly		Pet Friendly
	Store		Cafe		Firewood
	Ice		Security		Quiet	☐ Noisy

Laundry

😀 🙂 🙁 😠

Pool

😀 🙂 🙁 😠

GPS: _____

Altitude: _____

Cell Service/Carrier: _____

Hot tub

😀 🙂 🙁 😠

Wifi Available ○ Free ○ Fee $ _____

Memberships: _____

Amenities: _____

Overall rating

☆ ☆ ☆ ☆ ☆

Notes

_____

_____

Highlights & Favorite Things

_____

_____

Places & Activities:

_____

_____

_____

_____

_____

Contacts/New Friends

Name	Phone	E-mail	Mailing Address

Journal Page

Journal Page

List the NATIONAL Parks You Visit
(Name and State Abbreviation)

PARK NAME	ST	PARK NAME	ST

List the NATIONAL Parks You Visit
(Name and State Abbreviation)

PARK NAME	ST	PARK NAME	ST

List the STATE Parks You Visit
(Name and State Abbreviation)

PARK NAME	ST	PARK NAME	ST

List the STATE Parks You Visit
(Name and State Abbreviation)

PARK NAME	ST	PARK NAME	ST

Camping & Road Trip Bucket List

Place, State, and notes

X	NAME OF PLACE	ST	NOTES

Camping & Road Trip Bucket List

Place, State, and notes

X	NAME OF PLACE	ST	NOTES

Made in the USA
Columbia, SC
05 September 2022